汉语桥-中学生夏令营
Chinese Bridge Summer Camp for Foreign Students

中国欢迎你
Welcome to China
短期汉语系列教材

孔子学院总部/国家汉办
Institute Headquarters(Hanban)

You Beijing

游北京

Welcome to Beijing

修订版 Revised Edition

地域类

高等教育出版社·北京

“中国欢迎你”短期汉语系列教材

总策划　许　琳

总监制　王永利

策　划　陈　默　邵亦鹏

监　制　梁　宇　薛　佼

前言

为帮助“汉语桥—夏/冬令营”学生以及所有对中国感兴趣的外国朋友在较短时间内了解中国的语言与文化、历史与风俗，孔子学院总部/国家汉办组织研发，高等教育出版社于2011年正式出版发行了“中国欢迎你”短期汉语系列教材，受到了海内外教师和学生的普遍认可和喜爱。

为顺应汉语教学与文化体验项目的不断发展，孔子学院总部/国家汉办对教材使用情况开展了调研，编写组由此获得了教师和学生们对教材的宝贵反馈意见，对“中国欢迎你”短期汉语系列教材进行了系统修订和完善，精心研制并推出修订版。

适用对象

本系列教材主要适用于来华参加夏/冬令营的学生，海外孔子学院和孔子课堂也可将其用作教学辅助资源。

教材构成

本系列教材分为三大类：语言类、才艺类和地域类。

《游北京》是地域类教材中的一册，主要介绍北京的地域文化和风土人情，包括长城、故宫、天坛、前门大街、颐和园、购物天堂等。本书将地域文化的学习与参观游览有机地结合起来，同时配以丰富的练习和活动，目的在于让学习者在较短时间内了解北京、感知北京。本书的参考教学时间为6～8学时。

编写特色

1. 适用性：充分考虑海外青少年学习者短期学习的学习特点，以学习者为中心，合理设计教学内容和教学顺序，用深入浅出、图文并茂的方式展示汉语与文化。

2. 活动式：以任务和活动为主线，寓教于乐，注重实效，便于教师进行教学设计，充分调动学习者的学习兴趣，实现轻松有效的课堂教学。

3. 资源性：为教师和学习者提供各类丰富的素材，以及各类可以直接动手操作的练习，满足学习者的个性化需求。

让我们翻开书，一起去感知充满魅力的汉语和中国文化！

编委会

2016年2月

CONTENTS 目录

About Beijing
北京简介

Beijing, which is called "*Jing*" for short, is the capital of the People's Republic of China. It is the political, cultural and transportation center of the state. As a historical and cultural city, Beijing has a history of over 3 000 years as a city and a history of over 850 years as a capital, with many historical sites and other cultural places of interest. The old parts of city are characterized by the courtyard houses, or *siheyuan*, which line the narrow *hutongs* (alleyways) that Beijing is famous for. Old Beijingers have passed on many local customs, such as: Beijing snacks, Beijing Opera, cross-talk, cloisonné, blown-sugar figurines, flour figurines, and many other traditions. Beijing, an ancient capital with all the beauty of a fashionable city, is opening its arms wide to welcome friends from around the world.

北京，简称"京"，是中华人民共和国的首都，是中国政治、文化和交通中心。作为一座历史文化名城，北京有3 000余年的建城史和850余年的建都史，拥有众多的名胜古迹和人文景观。四合院是老北京城最主要的民居建筑，一座座四合院之间形成的窄巷就是著名的北京胡同。老北京人留下了很多颇具地方特色的民风习俗，如北京小吃、京剧、相声、景泰蓝、吹糖人、捏面人等。北京，这座古老而时尚的城市，正张开双臂欢迎来自世界各地的朋友们。

The Great Wall

长城

Warm-up 热身

1. Which of the following parts of the Great Wall were used for sending signals for military purposes in ancient times? Please tick the correct answer.

看图，猜猜在古代，长城上的哪种设施是用来传递军情的。请选择并画✓。

Garrison Town
关城
guānchéng

The Wall
城墙
chéngqiáng

Watchtower
烽火台
fēnghuǒtái

2. What do you know about the Great Wall? Please talk about it with your partner.

关于长城你都知道些什么？请跟同伴说一说。

- The Great Wall has a history of over 2 000 years.
- The Great Wall is located in the northern part of China.

◆ 长城 有 2 000 多 年的 历 史。
Chángchéng yǒu liǎngqiān duō nián de lìshǐ.

◆ 长城 在中国 的 北部。
Chángchéng zài Zhōngguó de běibù.

Did You Know? 你知道吗？

Have you ever seen the world's oldest, longest, most majestic "wall"? It is the Great Wall. The Great Wall, like the pyramids in Egypt and the Colosseum in Rome, is one of the "Seven Wonders of the World." The Wall dates back to between 700 BC and 500 BC. Since then the Great Wall has been repaired and expanded in many dynasties. The Great Wall runs across eight provinces in northern China, with a total length of about 13 000 *li* (6 700 km or 4 163 miles), so it is also called the "Ten Thousand *Li* Great Wall."

你见过世界上最古老、最长、最雄伟的"墙"吗？它就是长城。长城与埃及的金字塔、罗马的斗兽场等被誉为"世界七大奇迹"。最早修建的长城大约出现于公元前7世纪至公元前5世纪，此后许多朝代都对长城进行过修整和扩建。长城横穿中国北部8个省区市，全长约6 700千米，也就是13 000多华里，所以被称为"万里长城"。

Let's Think 想一想

1. How many years has the Great Wall been standing?
   长城已有多少年的历史了？
2. How long is the Great Wall?
   长城有多长？

The Badaling Great Wall 八达岭长城

The Badaling Great Wall is situated northwest of Beijing and was built along the mountain ridges. It was the northern gateway to the capital city Beijing during the Ming Dynasty, and played an important role in military affairs.

八达岭长城位于北京的西北部，依山而建，明朝时期是京城的北大门，在军事上的地位非常重要。

Jiayuguan 嘉峪关

Jiayuguan, or the Jiayu Pass, is located in Gansu province and is the western terminus of the Great Wall. It is also known as “the Most Impregnable Pass in the World”.

嘉峪关在甘肃省境内，是长城最西端的关隘，有“天下雄关”之称。

Shanhaiguan 山海关

Shanhaiguan, or the Shanhai Pass, is situated in the city of Qinhuangdao in Heibei province. It is nicknamed “the World’s Number One Pass”.

山海关位于河北省秦皇岛市境内，有“天下第一关”之称。

At the back of your book, you can find stickers of Jiayuguan and Shanhaiguan. Stick them in the correct places.

Jiayuguan

Shanhaiguan

Useful Expressions 常用表达

1. 请问，这是什么？
   Qǐng wèn, zhè shì shénme?
2. 这是做什么用的？
   Zhè shì zuò shénme yòng de?
3. 太累了！
   Tài lèi le!
4. 休息一下吧！
   Xiūxi yíxià ba!
5. 加油！
   Jiāyóu!

1. Excuse me, what is this?
2. What is this used for?
3. I'm really exhausted!
4. Let's rest a bit!
5. Come on!

Tasks 任务

1 Measure how thick a brick from the Great Wall is, and write down your answer in the space below.
测量一下一块长城的砖有多厚，把答案写在下面的空格里。

2 Draw some of the Great Wall from what you have seen.
画出一段你看到的长城。

The Palace Museum

故 宫

Warm-up 热身

1 The following pictures all show something from inside the Palace Museum. Guess what they were used for and dissuss them with your partner.

看图，猜猜这些故宫里的东西是做什么用的。请跟同伴讨论一下。

① 日晷 rìguǐ

② 嘉量 jiāliàng

③ 龙头 lóngtóu

I think *rigui* was used for ________.
我猜日晷是用来________的。

2 Does your country have things like those in the pictures above? What are they? Tell your classmates about them.

你们国家有类似上图中的东西吗？是什么？跟大家说一说。

Did You Know?

你知道吗？

In the center of Beijing, there is a large group of ancient wooden buildings which make up the Palace Museum. It is also called the "Forbidden City". It is one of the world's five largest palaces. For around 600 years, the Ming and Qing Emperors worked and lived within these buildings. The Palace Museum covers an area of 720 000 m^2, encircled by 10 meters high and 3 400 meters long walls, with 52 meters wide moat around the outside. The magnificent Palace Museum, with its North-South alignment and symmetrical layout, is the essence of ancient Chinese architectural art.

在北京城的中心，有一座规模庞大的木质结构古建筑群，它就是北京故宫，又名“紫禁城”。作为世界五大宫殿之一，这座约有600年历史的宫殿曾经是明、清两代皇帝工作和生活的地方。故宫的占地面积为72万多平方米，周围有高10米、长3 400米的宫墙，墙外有52米宽的护城河环绕。故宫宫殿南北取直，左右对称，是中国古代建筑艺术的精华。

Let's Think 想一想

1. How long is the history of the Palace Museum?
   故宫有多少年的历史了？
2. What are the characteristics of the architecture of the Palace Museum?
   故宫在建筑风格方面有什么特点？

The Porcelain of the Palace Museum 故宫的瓷器

The Palace Museum contains a collection of 1.5 million cultural relics, 350 000 of which are porcelain. The most remarkable piece is an 87 cm high porcelain vase, which is called the "the mother of Porcelain".

故宫现在藏有约150万件文物，其中约35万件是瓷器，最令人瞩目的是一件高87厘米的大瓷瓶，被称为“瓷母”。

The Mother of Porcelain

At the back of your book, you can find a sticker of the "the mother of Porcelain". Stick it in the correct place.

Useful Expressions 常用表达

1. 这是什么建筑？
   Zhè shì shénme jiànzhù?
2. 太美了！
   Tài měi le!
3. 这件文物有多少年的历史了？
   Zhè jiàn wénwù yǒu duōshao nián de lìshǐ le?
4. 你能帮我拍张照片吗？
   Nǐ néng bāng wǒ pāi zhāng zhàopiàn ma?
5. 请问，卫生间在哪里？
   Qǐng wèn, wèishēngjiān zài nǎlǐ?

1. What is this building?
2. It is so beautiful!
3. How long is the history of this cultural relic?
4. Can you help me take a photo?
5. Excuse me, where is the washroom?

Tasks 任务

1. Work in groups and discuss the picture on the right. What was this large vat used for? See which group is the first to guess the correct answer.
   几人一组，讨论一下右图中的大缸原来是做什么用的。看看哪组最先猜出正确答案。

2. Try to find the following places and take a picture at each place.
   在故宫里找找下面几个地方，并分别在各处拍一张照片。

3. When visiting the Palace Museum, please observe the lions in front of the door of many palaces. Do you know which one is the male and which one is the female? How can you tell?
   参观故宫的时候，请仔细观察宫殿门口的狮子。你能分辨出哪只是公的，哪只是母的吗？你是怎么知道的？

The Temple of Heaven

天 坛

Warm-up 热身

1. Which of the following sentences is an ancient Chinese saying? Is this saying correct? Why or why not?
下面哪个是古代中国人的想法？这种想法对吗？为什么？

- The sky is round, the earth is square.
天圆地方。

- The earth is round.
地球是圆的。

2. The picture of the stone below is the "Three Echo Stones" in the Temple of Heaven. Do you know why it is called the "Three Echo Stones"? Please discuss it with your partner.
下面的石板是天坛里的"三音石"。你知道它为什么叫"三音石"吗？请跟同伴讨论一下。

Did You Know? 你知道吗？

The Temple of Heaven is the largest altar temple compound in China. In ancient China, the Temple of Heaven was a sacred place. It was where Emperors of the Ming and Qing Dynasties offered sacrifices to heaven and prayed for good harvests. The Temple of Heaven includes many amazing buildings. For example, the Hall of Prayer for Good Harvests is a circular building which has a diameter of 32.72 meters and is 38 meters high. It was built entirely of wood, using a sub-tenon joint construction, meaning that no nails were used to hold it together.

天坛是中国现存最大的坛庙建筑，原来是明、清两代皇帝祭天和祈祷丰收的地方，在古代中国具有无比神圣的地位。天坛里有许多神奇的建筑。祈年殿是一座直径32.72米的圆形建筑，总高38米，却没有使用一个钉子，完全是靠木头榫子建造起来的。

***Let's Think* 想一想**

What did the Emperors of ancient China do at the Temple of Heaven?
中国古代皇帝去天坛做什么？

The Echo Wall 回音壁

The Echo Wall has an echoing effect. If two people stand at distant places and face the northern wall, one person talks quietly and the other person puts his/her ear close to the wall, he/she can hear the first person very clearly. Also, he/she can hear the echo of the sound for a long time.

天坛的“回音壁”有回音的效果。相距很远的两个人，同时面朝北墙，一个人轻声说话，另一个人把耳朵贴在墙上，就可以清楚地听见同伴所说的话，而且回音悠长。

Let's Think 想一想

Give an example of an amazing building that is found at the Temple of Heaven.
举例说说天坛里神奇的建筑。

Useful Expressions 常用表达

1. 快点儿，要迟到了。
   Kuài diǎnr, yào chídào le.
2. 我不是大学生，我是高中生。
   Wǒ bú shì dàxuéshēng, wǒ shì gāozhōngshēng.
3. 我很喜欢这里。
   Wǒ hěn xǐhuan zhèlǐ.
4. 太有意思了！
   Tài yǒuyìsi le!

1. Hurry up! We are going to be late.
2. I am not a university student. I am a middle school student.
3. I really like this place.
4. It's so interesting!

Tasks 任务

1 Stand in the center of the Circular Mound Altar and say a sentence loudly in Chinese. Write what you said in the space below.

站在天坛圜丘坛的天心石上用汉语大声说一句话，把你说的话写在下面的空格里。

2 A small experiment at the Echo Wall: one person faces the northern wall and says something in Chinese. The other person puts his ear to the wall. How softly can you speak and still hear the sound? How do you get the best sound effect?

回音壁小实验：一个人面朝北墙说中文，另一个人把耳朵贴在墙上，测试一下声音低到什么程度仍能听到，在什么情况下声音效果最好。

3 How many columns does the Hall of Prayer for Good Harvests have? What do they represent? Draw your answer below.

祈年殿里一共有多少根柱子？它们分别代表了什么？请画图说明。

Qianmen Street

前门大街

Warm-up 热身

1 Which of the following pictures is Qianmen Street? Please tick the correct answer.
下面哪幅图片是前门大街？请选择并画✓。

2 On Qianmen Street, there is a kind of railroad car called the "Clang Clang Car". Read the name of the vehicle several times with the teacher and guess why it is called the "Clang Clang Car".
在前门大街，有一种有轨电车叫"铛铛车"。请跟老师读几遍这种车的名字，并猜一猜它为什么叫"铛铛车"。

铛铛车
Dāngdāng Chē

Did You Know? 你知道吗？

Qianmen Street is one of Beijing's most famous shopping streets. It is more than 800 meters long and it already has a history of over 500 years. There are a lot of well-known shops on Qianmen street, dozens of which are well-reputed brands nationwide. Most of these branded shops are located in a short 200-meter section called "*Dashilanr*". Old Beijingers have a saying: "To see things, go to *Tianqiao*, to buy things, go to *Dashilanr*." From this, you can see the popularity and prosperity of *Dashilanr* in the old days.

前门大街是北京最著名的商业步行街之一。它全长800多米，至今已有500多年的历史。前门的商户不仅数量多，而且名气大，全国闻名的老字号有十几家，主要集中在只有短短200多米长的"大栅栏"商业街上。老北京人有句顺口溜叫"看玩意儿上天桥，买东西去大栅栏"，由此可见"大栅栏"在老北京人心中的地位及其旧日的繁华景象。

大栅栏 Dàshílànr

Time-honored Brands 老字号

Liubiju, established in 1530, is famous for salty vegetables.
六必居，始于1530年，以酱菜闻名。

Tongrentang, established in 1669, is a famous brand in the Chinese medicinal industry.
同仁堂，始于1669年，是中药行业著名的老字号。

Majuyuan, established in 1817, is a famous shop for selling hats.
马聚源，始于1817年，是以出售帽子为主的店铺。

Neiliansheng, established in 1853, is a famous shop for making shoes.
内联升，始于1853年，是以生产鞋子而闻名的店铺。

Ruifuxiang, established in 1893, is mainly famous for selling silks.
瑞蚨祥，始于1893年，主要以经营绸缎布匹而闻名。

Zhangyiyuan, established in 1900, is a famous tea seller in Beijing.
张一元，始于1900年，是京城经营茶叶的著名商户。

Let's Think 想一想

1. Which time-honored brands on Qianmen Street are related to clothing and hats?
   在前门，与穿戴有关的北京老字号有哪几家？
2. Which time-honored brands are you interested in most? Why?
   你最感兴趣的北京老字号是哪一家？为什么？

At the back of your book, you can find stickers of Majuyuan, Zhangyiyuan and Neiliansheng. Stick them in the correct places.

Majuyuan

Zhangyiyuan

Neiliansheng

Useful Expressions 常用表达

1. 请问，哪里可以买到帽子？
   Qǐng wèn, nǎlǐ kěyǐ mǎi dào màozi?
2. 这双鞋多少钱？
   Zhè shuāng xié duōshao qián?
3. 太贵了！便宜一点儿吧。
   Tài guì le! Piányi yìdiǎnr ba.

1. Excuse me, where can I buy a hat?
2. How much is this pair of shoes?
3. Too expensive! Could you give me a lower price?

Tasks 任务

1. Try the "Clang Clang Car" on Qianmen Street. How much does it cost? How long does it take from the first station to the terminal? Write your answer below.
   在前门大街坐一次“铛铛车”。车票的价格是多少？走完全程一共用了多长时间？

2. Stroll around Qianmen Street and buy some souvenirs for your family and friends. Note down the names of the souvenirs and their prices.
   逛一逛前门大街，给你的家人或朋友买几件纪念品。在下面的空格里写出纪念品的名称及价钱。

The Summer Palace

颐和园

Warm-up 热身

1 What do you know about the Summer Palace? Work with a partner to decide whether the following statements about the Summer Palace are true or false. Place a tick next to them if they are true, and a cross if they are false.

关于颐和园你都知道些什么？请跟同伴一起判断下列关于颐和园的信息，正确的画✓，不正确的画✗。

- The Summer Palace is one of the world's most famous royal parks.
  颐和园是世界最著名的皇家园林之一。
- The Summer Palace is the largest royal park in China.
  颐和园是中国面积最大的皇家园林。
- The Summer Palace was built during the Qing dynasty, China's last feudal dynasty.
  颐和园是中国最后一个封建王朝清朝时建的。
- The Summer Palace is located in the East of Beijing.
  颐和园在北京的东边。
- Kunming Lake is a natural lake.
  昆明湖是一个天然湖泊。

Did You Know? 你知道吗？

The site of the Summer Palace was originally called Qingyi Garden, which was a large Imperial garden built in 1750 by the Qing dynasty emperor, Qianlong, to mark the celebration of his mother's 60th birthday. The Summer Palace is situated surrounding Kunming Lake and Longevity Hill, designed with the Southern Chinese style of Hangzhou's West Lake as its blueprint. It is also known as the "Imperial Park Museum". The Summer Palace is China's largest and best-preserved Imperial park and, along with the Emperor's summer hillside retreat in Chengde, the Humble Administrator's Garden, and the Lingering Garden in Suzhou, is recognized as one of the country's four most famous parks.

颐和园原名为清漪园，始建于公元1750年，是清朝乾隆皇帝为其母亲庆祝60寿辰而建造的一座大型皇家园林。颐和园是以昆明湖、万寿山为基址，以杭州西湖为蓝本，汲取江南园林的设计手法而建成的，被称为“皇家园林博物馆”。颐和园也是保存最完整、面积最大的一座皇家行宫御苑，与承德避暑山庄、苏州的拙政园和留园并称为中国四大名园。

Kumming Lake 昆明湖

Kunming Lake accounts for three quarters of the area of the Summer Palace, and is the largest lake in any of the Qing dynasty Imperial parks.

昆明湖占颐和园面积的四分之三，是清代皇家诸园中最大的湖泊。

Longevity Hill 万寿山

The summit of Longevity Hill is 60 meters high and recognizable for its numerous Buddhist temples and pavilions.

万寿山（高60米）上有著名的佛香阁排云殿建筑群。

The Long Gallery 长廊

The Summer Palace is also famous for its beautiful Long Gallery, which is a wooden walkway covered in intricate painted patterns and designs.

颐和园同时以美丽的长廊著称，长廊是一条绘有精致图画的木制走廊。

Useful Expressions 常用表达

1. 游览长廊需要多长时间？
Yóulǎn Chánglóng xūyào duō cháng shíjiān?

2. 我们走着去还是坐船去？
Wǒmen zǒuzhe qù háishi zuò chuán qù?

1. How long does it take to walk along the Long Gallery?

2. Shall we walk there or take a boat?

Tasks 任务

Find the places below at the Summer Palace, and take a photo in each place.

在颐和园找到下面几个地方，并分别在各处拍一张照片。

Shopping Paradise

购物天堂

Beijing boasts many good shopping areas. In *Panjiayuan* or *Nan Luoguxiang*, you can find Chinese traditional specialty products that you want. In *Wangfujing*, *Xidan* or *Sanlitun*, there is a huge variety of unique and stylish products. You could say that if you can't find what you want to buy in Beijing, then you can't buy it anywhere.

北京有很多购物的好去处。在潘家园、南锣鼓巷，你可以找到具有中国特色的商品。在王府井、西单、三里屯，有多种多样的时尚、充满个性的商品。总之，在北京，只有你想不到的，没有你买不到的。

Useful Expressions 常用表达

1. 这件衣服多少钱？
   Zhè jiàn yīfu duōshao qián?
2. 太贵了！便宜一点儿吧。
   Tài guì le! Piányi yìdiǎnr ba.
3. 能不能再便宜点儿？
   Néng bu néng zài piányi diǎnr?

1. How much is this item of clothing?
2. Too expensive! Could you go a little lower on the price?
3. Can you go even lower on the price?

Some Shopping Tips

1. When you are at wholesale markets, you must ask and compare several stores before deciding which shop to buy from. Don't make any quick decisions, especially when purchasing high-price items.
2. Ask the shop owner whether they can give you a discount or not before you start bargaining. Be patient and you will get the item you want at the right price.

Hongqiao Market 红桥市场

Hongqiao Market is the world's largest pearl retail market. Inside the market, on the first and second floors there are numerous businesses with products including digital products, watches, clothing, bags, silk, small merchandise and many other items. Stores selling pearl products are located on the third, fourth and fifth floors.

红桥市场是目前全球最大的珍珠零售市场。市场楼内的1—2层经营数码产品、手表、服装、箱包、丝绸、小百货等，3—5层均为珍珠产品销售区域。

Tasks 任务

1. Walk around Hongqiao Market and find the kind of product you like most and then find your favorite store. Write down these names in the spaces below.
逛逛红桥市场，找出你最喜欢的一类商品和一家店铺，把它们的名称写在下面的空格里。

2. Have a look at the pearl products at Hongqiao Market and complete the following tasks.
考察一下红桥市场的珍珠产品，完成下面的任务。

(1) How much was the cheapest pearl necklace you saw?
你见到的最便宜的珍珠项链是多少钱？

(2) How much was the most expensive pearl necklace you saw?
你见到的最贵的珍珠项链是多少钱？

(3) Take a photo of the pearl necklace that you thought was the most beautiful.
为你认为最漂亮的珍珠项链拍一张照片。

Panjiayuan Curio Market 潘家园旧货市场

Panjiayuan Curio Market is the most popular and flourishing antique curio market in China. It is also the largest folk handicraft distribution center in China. There are more than 4 000 shops, and they primarily sell antique goods, handicrafts, collectors' items and decorations, among other things.

潘家园旧货市场是中国人气最旺的古旧物品市场，也是中国最大的民间工艺品集散地。这里共有4 000余家商户，主营古旧物品、工艺品、收藏品和装饰品等。

Tasks 任务

1 Work in pairs. Go to Panjiayuan Curio Market and find examples like those seen in the pictures below. Take photos of what you find. Within 30 minutes, see which pair can complete this task the fastest and the best.

两人一组，在潘家园旧货市场找到下列图片中的同类物品，并拍照。规定时间为30分钟，看哪组完成得又快又好。

cloisonné
景泰蓝
jǐngtàilán

comic books
连环画
liánhuánhuà

porcelain
瓷器
cíqì

small bag
荷包
hébāo

ancient coins
古钱币
gǔ qiánbì

wooden carvings and sculptures
木雕
mùdiāo

jade ware
玉器
yùqì

purple clay teapot
紫砂壶
zǐshāhú

2 Go to Panjiayuan Curio Market and use 50 *yuan* to buy something with an asking price of 300 *yuan*. When you go back to class, show what you bought to your classmates and introduce how you bargained for it.

在潘家园用50元钱购买要价300元的物品。上课时向全班同学展示买到的物品并介绍讲价过程。

Wangfujing Street 王府井大街

Wangfujing Street is called the "First Commercial Street in China". It is 1 600 meters long altogether and has a history of more than 700 years. Here you can find all of the famous international brands, as well as many time-honored Chinese brands. You can also savour delicious and unique Beijing delicacies.

王府井大街被称为“中华第一商业街”，全长1 600米，至今已有700多年的历史。这里既有各大国际知名品牌，也有历史悠久的中华老字号，还可以品尝风味独特的北京美食。

Tasks 任务

1 Along Wangfujing Street, find the shops shown below and find out what business they deal in.
在王府井大街上找到下面几家店铺，并考察一下这些店铺分别经营什么。

2 Along Wangfujing Street, look for international brand-name stores and take photos in front of them. Within 30 minutes, see who can complete this task the fastest and the best.
在王府井大街上找找国际知名品牌店，并拍照留念。规定时间为30分钟，看谁完成得又快又好。

Answers 答 案

The Great Wall
长城

1.  Watchtower 烽火台 P2

1. The Great Wall has a history of over 2 000 years. 长城已有2 000多年的历史了。
2. The Great Wall has a total length of 13 000 *li* (6 700 km or 4 163 miles). 长城全长约6 700千米，也就是13 000多华里。 P3

The Palace Museum
故宫

1. ① *Rigui* is a kind of instrument that ancient Chinese people used to measure the time, using the sun and shadows. 日晷是中国古代利用日影测得时刻的一种计时仪器。
   ② *Jialiang* is the standard of Chinese ancient measuring devices. 嘉量是中国古代的标准量具。
   ③ *Longtou* is a type of drainage equipment. 龙头是一种排水设施。 P6

1. The Palace Museum has a history of over 600 years. 故宫有600年的历史了。
2. The Palace Museum is noted for its North-South alignment and symmetrical layout. 故宫宫殿南北取直，左右对称。 P7

1. The large vat is full of water which can be used to put out a fire. 大缸里面盛满了水，是用来防火的。
3. The male lion steps on a ball and the female lion steps on a small lion. 公狮子脚下踩一个球，母狮子脚下踩一只小狮子。 P9

The Temple of Heaven
天坛

1. People in ancient China thought that the sky was round and the earth was square. We now know that this thought is incorrect. 古代中国人认为：天圆地方。这种想法是不对的。 P10

Emperors of the Ming and Qing Dynasties offered sacrifices to heaven and prayed for good harvests at the Temple of Heaven. 明、清两代皇帝去天坛祭天和祈祷丰收。 P11

3. The Hall of Prayer for Good Harvests has 28 pillars. The center 4 represent the four seasons. The middle 12 represent the twelve months. The outside 12 represent the twelve two-hour periods of the day. The middle and the outside ones added together, totalling 24, represent the 24 solar terms, and the three layers added together, totalling 28, represent the 28 star constellations. 祈年殿有28根大柱。中央四根代表四季，中层12根代表12个月，外层12根代表12时辰，中外层相加24根代表24节气，三层相加28根代表28星宿。 P13

Qianmen Street
前门大街

1. 

2. Because there is a small copper bell hanging in the front of the Clang Clang Car, the driver only has to put his or her feet down to press the brake pedal, and the bell will start to make a "clang clang" sound, alerting the pedestrians to move out of the way of the car. 因为铛铛车的车头挂了一只铜铃铛，司机只要一踩脚下的踏板，铃铛便会发出"铛铛"的声响，提醒行人闪避车辆。 P14

1. *Ruifuxiang*, *Majuyuan* and *Neiliansheng*. P16

The Summer Palace
颐和园

1. ✓ 2. ✓ 3. ✓ 4. ✗ 5. ✓ P18

图书在版编目（CIP）数据

中国欢迎你. 游北京 / 孔子学院总部 / 国家汉办编著
. -- 2版（修订本）. -- 北京：高等教育出版社，
2016.6（2018.12重印）
“中国欢迎你”短期汉语系列教材
ISBN 978-7-04-044992-1

Ⅰ. ①中… Ⅱ. ①孔… Ⅲ. ①汉语－对外汉语教学－
教材 Ⅳ. ①H195.4

中国版本图书馆CIP数据核字（2016）第048071号

策划编辑 鞠 慧　责任编辑 鞠 慧 杨 曦　封面设计 乔 剑　版式设计 三月天地
英文审译 Simon Golding　插图选配 杨 曦　责任校对 杨 曦　责任印制 田 甜

出版发行 高等教育出版社
社 址 北京市西城区德外大街4号
邮政编码 100120
印 刷 北京信彩瑞禾印刷厂
开 本 787mm×1092mm 1/16
印 张 2
字 数 50千字
购书热线 010-58581118
咨询电话 400-810-0598
网 址 http://www.hep.edu.cn
http://www.hep.com.cn
网上订购 http://www.hepmall.com.cn
http://www.hepmall.com
http://www.hepmall.cn
版 次 2011年6月第1版
2016年6月第2版
印 次 2018年12月第4次印刷
定 价 13.80元

物 料 号 44992-00